Veterinarian

Career Assessments and Their Meanings

Childcare Worker

Clergy

Computer Programmer

Financial Advisor

Firefighter

Homeland Security Officer

Journalist

Manager

Military and Elite Forces Officer

Nurse

Politician

Professional Athlete and Sports Official

Psychologist

Research Scientist

Social Worker

Special Education Teacher

Veterinarian

Careers with Character

Veterinarian

by John Riddle and Rae Simons

MASON CREST PUBLISHERS

Mason Crest Publishers Inc.
370 Reed Road
Broomall, Pennsylvania 19008
(866) MCP-BOOK (toll free)
www.masoncrest.com

First printing
1 2 3 4 5 6 7 8 9 10
Library of Congress Cataloging-in-Publication Data on file at the Library of Congress.
ISBN 1-59084-326-6
        1-59084-327-4 (series)

Design by Lori Holland.
Composition by Bytheway Publishing Services, Binghamton, New York.
Printed and bound in the Hashemite Kingdom of Jordan.

Photo Credits:
Comstock: pp. 16, 18, 20, 44, 46, 47, 49, 60, 62, 63, 64, 65, 68, 70, 72, 73, 76, 80, 82
Corbis: pp. 29, 30, 31, cover
Corel: pp. 4, 8, 21, 24, 26, 28, 34, 36, 37, 39, 48, 52, 55, 56, 79
PhotoDisc: pp. 6, 11, 12, 54, 57, 71

CONTENTS

We each leave a fingerprint on the world.
Our careers are the work we do in life.
Our characters are shaped by the choices
we make to do good.
When we combine careers with character,
we touch the world with power.

INTRODUCTION

by Dr. Cheryl Gholar
and Dr. Ernestine G. Riggs

In today's world, the awesome task of choosing or staying in a career has become more involved than one would ever have imagined in past decades. Whether the job market is robust or the demand for workers is sluggish, the need for top-performing employees with good character remains a priority on most employers' lists of "must have" or "must keep." When critical decisions are being made regarding a company or organization's growth or future, job performance and work ethic are often the determining factors as to who will remain employed and who will not.

How does one achieve success in one's career and in life? Victor Frankl, the Austrian psychologist, summarized the concept of success in the preface to his book *Man's Search for Meaning* as: "The unintended side-effect of one's personal dedication to a course greater than oneself." Achieving value by responding to life and careers from higher levels of knowing and being is a specific goal of teaching and learning in "Careers with Character." What constitutes success for us as individuals can be found deep within our belief system. Seeking, preparing, and attaining an excellent career that aligns with our personality is an outstanding goal. However, an excellent career augmented by exemplary character is a visible expression of the human need to bring meaning, purpose, and value to our work.

Career education informs us of employment opportunities, occupational outlooks, earnings, and preparation needed to perform certain tasks. Character education provides insight into how a person of good character might choose to respond, initiate an action, or perform specific tasks in the presence of an ethical dilemma. "Careers with Character" combines the two and teaches students that careers are more than just jobs. Career development is incomplete without character development. What better way to explore careers and character than to make them a single package to be opened, examined, and reflected upon as a means of understanding the greater whole of who we are and what work can mean when one chooses to become an employee of character?

Character can be defined simply as "who you are even when no one else is around." Your character is revealed by your choices and actions. These bear your personal signature, validating the story of who you are. They are the fingerprints you leave behind on the people you meet and know; they are the ideas you bring into reality. Your choices tell the world what you truly believe.

Character, when viewed as a standard of excellence, reminds us to ask ourselves when choosing a career: "Why this particular career, for what purpose, and to what end?" The authors of "Careers with Character" knowledgeably and passionately, through their various vignettes, enable one to experience an inner journey that is both intellectual and moral. Students will find themselves, when confronting decisions in real life, more prepared, having had experiential learning opportunities through this series. The books, however, do not separate or negate the individual good from the academic skills or intellect needed to perform the required tasks that lead to productive career development and personal fulfillment.

Each book is replete with exemplary role models, practical strategies, instructional tools, and applications. In each volume, individuals of character work toward ethical leadership, learning how to respond appropriately to issues of not only right versus wrong, but issues of right versus right, understanding the possible benefits and consequences of their decisions. A wealth of examples is provided.

What is it about a career that moves our hearts and minds toward fulfilling a dream? It is our character. The truest approach to finding out who we are and what illuminates our lives is to look within. At the very heart of career development is good character. At the heart of good character is an individual who knows and loves the good, and seeks to share the good with others. By exploring careers and character together, we create internal and external environments that support and enhance each other, challenging students to lead conscious lives of personal quality and true richness every day.

Is there a difference between doing the right thing, and doing things right? Career questions ask, "What do you know about a specific career?" Character questions ask, "Now that you know about a specific career, what will you choose to do with what you know?" "How will you perform certain tasks and services for others, even when no one else is around?" "Will all individuals be given your best regardless of their socioeconomic background, physical condition, ethnicity, or religious beliefs?" Character questions often challenge the authenticity of what we say we believe and value in the workplace and in our personal lives.

Character and career questions together challenge us to pay attention to our lives and not fall asleep on the job. Career knowledge, self-knowledge, and ethical wisdom help us answer deeper questions about the meaning of work; they give us permission to transform our lives. Personal integrity is the price of admission.

The insight of one "ordinary" individual can make a difference in the world—if that one individual believes that character is an amazing gift to uncap knowledge and talents to empower the human community. Our world needs everyday heroes in the workplace—and "Careers with Character" challenges students to become those heroes.

This fawn is cute—but it takes more than a love of animals to become a good veterinarian.

1

JOB REQUIREMENTS

If you want to be a veterinarian, education is one requirement for success—and a good character is another.

You are sitting at your desk, trying to eat lunch as you read *Veterinary News*, a trade journal, when your nurse rushes in to tell you that someone has just brought in a cat that was hit by a car. Suddenly that tuna fish sandwich no longer seems important; your job as a veterinarian is to treat animals and to save their lives, and you are ready to help a cat who is in trouble. Thirty minutes later, you breathe easier when you realize the cat will be okay. As a veterinarian, you must always be prepared for emergencies. The lives of innocent animals depend upon you.

The art of veterinary medicine can be traced back to India, when in 1800 B.C. people started recording descriptions of doctors treating animals. It wasn't until A.D. 1762, however, that the first government-sponsored school of veterinary medicine was established in Lyons, France. In the United States, the federal government created the United States Department of Agriculture (USDA) in 1862. That led to the first public-supported college of veterinary medicine in 1879 at Iowa State College.

Today, veterinarians play a major role in the healthcare of pets, livestock, and zoo, sporting, and laboratory animals. Some veterinarians use their skills to protect humans against diseases carried by animals and conduct clinical research on human and animal health problems. Others work in basic research, broadening the scope of fundamental theoretical knowledge, and in applied research, developing new ways to use knowledge.

Veterinarians who treat animals use medical equipment, such as stethoscopes; surgical instruments; and diagnostic equipment, such as radiographic and ultra-sound equipment. Veterinarians working in research use a full range of sophisticated laboratory equipment.

Most veterinarians perform clinical work in private practices. More than a half of these veterinarians treat small animals. Small animal practitioners usually care for companion animals, such as dogs and cats, but they also treat birds, reptiles, rabbits, and other animals

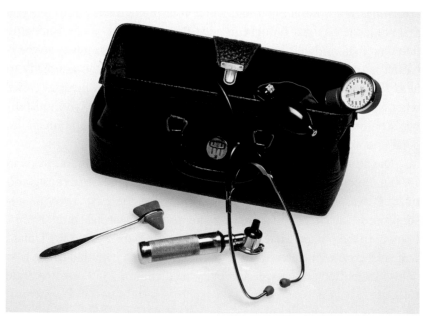

Veterinarians use many of the same instruments as doctors.

In Canada, the degree Doctor of Veterinary Medicine (DVM) requires a minimum of six years of university education: two years of preveterinary study at a regular university followed by four years of courses in veterinary medicine at one of the four Canadian veterinary colleges. The number of students that can be accommodated in a veterinary school is limited; all the Canadian veterinary colleges combined currently graduate only about 400 veterinarians each year.

that can be kept as pets. Some veterinarians work in mixed animal practices where they see pigs, goats, sheep, and some nondomestic animals, in addition to companion animals. Veterinarians in clinical practice diagnose animal health problems; vaccinate against diseases, such as distemper and rabies; medicate animals suffering from infections or illnesses; treat and dress wounds; set fractures; perform surgery; and advise owners about animal feeding, behavior, and breeding.

A small number of private practice veterinarians work exclusively with large animals, focusing mostly on horses or cows, but they may also care for various kinds of food animals. These veterinarians usually drive to farms or ranches to provide veterinary services for herds or individual animals. Much of this work involves preventive care to maintain the health of the food animals. These veterinarians test for and vaccinate against diseases and consult with farm or ranch owners and managers on animal production, feeding, and housing issues. They also treat and dress wounds, set fractures, and perform surgery, including *cesarean sections* on birthing animals. Veterinarians also *euthanize* animals when necessary. Other veterinarians care for zoo, aquarium, or laboratory animals.

Veterinarians often work long hours, with well over one-third of full-time workers spending 50 or more hours a week on the job. Those in group practices may take turns being on call for evening, night, or weekend work; and solo practitioners can work extended and weekend hours, responding to emergencies or squeezing in unexpected appointments.

Many veterinarians work with large farm animals.

Professionals in large-animal practice also spend time driving between their office and farms or ranches. They work outdoors in all kinds of weather, and have to treat animals or perform surgery under less-than-sanitary conditions. When working with animals that are frightened or in pain, veterinarians risk being bitten, kicked, or scratched.

Those veterinarians who work in nonclinical areas, however, such as public health and research, have working conditions similar to those of other professionals in similar lines of work. In these cases, veterinarians enjoy clean, well-lit offices or laboratories and spend much of their time dealing with people rather than animals. Prospective veterinarians must graduate from a four-year program at an accredited college of veterinary medicine with a Doctor of Veterinary Medicine (DVM or VMD) degree and obtain a license to practice. There are 27 colleges in the United States that meet accreditation standards set by the Council on Education of the American Veterinary Medical Association. The prerequisites for admission vary by veterinary medical college. Many of these colleges do not require a bachelor's degree for entrance, but all require a significant number of credit hours—ranging from 45 to 90 semester hours—at the undergraduate level. Most of the students admitted have completed an undergraduate program.

Preveterinary courses emphasize the sciences; and veterinary medical colleges typically require classes in organic and inorganic chemistry, physics, biochemistry, general biology, animal biology, animal nutrition, genetics, vertebrate embryology, cellular biology, microbiology, zoology, and systemic physiology. Some programs require calculus; some require only statistics, college algebra and trigonometry, or precalculus; and others require no math at all. Most veterinary medical colleges also require core courses, including some in English or literature, the social sciences, and the humanities.

Most veterinary medical colleges will only consider applicants who have a minimum grade point average (GPA); the required GPA varies by school, from a low of 2.5 to a high of 3.2, based on a maximum GPA of 4.0. However, the average GPA of candidates at most schools is higher than these minimums. Those who receive offers of admission usually have a GPA of 3.0 or better.

In addition to satisfying preveterinary course requirements, applicants must also submit test scores from the Graduate Record Examination (GRE), the Veterinary College Admission Test (VCAT), or the Medical College Admission Test (MCAT), depending on the preference of each college.

> If you want to be a vet, you will need:
>
> • an inquiring and studious mind.
> • to keep up on new development and techniques in veterinary medicine.
> • to have the confidence to handle animals who are sick and injured.
> • to have good communication skills for speaking with animal owners and other professionals.

Additionally, in the admissions process, veterinary medical colleges weigh heavily a candidate's veterinary and animal experience. Formal experience, such as work with veterinarians or scientists in clinics, ***agribusiness***, research, or in some area of health science, is particularly advantageous. Less formal experience, such as working with animals on a farm or ranch or at a stable or animal shelter, is also helpful. Students must demonstrate ambition and an eagerness to work with animals.

The competition for admission to veterinary school is keen. The number of accredited veterinary colleges has remained at 27 since 1983, whereas the number of applicants has risen; only about one in three applicants was accepted in 1998. Most veterinary medical colleges are public, state-supported institutions and reserve the majority of their openings for in-state residents. Twenty-one states that do not have a veterinary medical college agree to pay a fee or subsidy to help cover the cost of veterinary education for a limited number of their residents at one or more out-of-state colleges. Nonresident students who are admitted under such a contract may have to pay out-of-state tuition, or they may have to repay their state of residency all or part of the subsidy provided to the contracting college. Residents of the remaining three states (Connecticut, Maine, and Vermont) and the District of Columbia may apply to any of the 27 veterinary medical colleges as an "at-large" applicant. The number of positions available to at-large applicants is very limited at most schools, making admission difficult.

While in veterinary medical college, students receive additional academic instruction in the basic sciences for the first two years. Later in

If you are interested in a career in veterinary medicine, a good book to look for in the library is called *Veterinary Guide for Animal Owners,* by Jackie Clay and C. E. Spaulding. It is published by Rodale Publishing, and it will give you some insight into how to care for animals. It has complete chapters on cats, cows, dogs, goats, horses, pigs, and dozens of other animals. No matter what career choice you are making in life, it is always a good idea to read as many books on the subject as you can.

Students in veterinary medical colleges will study research methods.

the program, students experience clinical procedures, such as diagnosing and treating animal diseases and performing surgery. They also perform laboratory work in anatomy, biochemistry, medicine, and other scientific subjects. At most veterinary medical colleges, students who plan a career in research can earn both a DVM degree and a Doctor of Philosophy (PhD) degree at the same time.

Veterinary graduates who plan to work with specific types of animals or specialize in a clinical area, such as pathology, surgery, radiology, or laboratory animal medicine, usually complete a one-year internship. Interns receive a small salary but usually find that their internship experience leads to a higher beginning salary, relative to other starting veterinarians. Veterinarians who seek board certification in a specialty must also complete a two- to three-year residency program that provides intensive training in specialties such as internal medicine, oncology, radiology, surgery, dermatology, anesthesiology, neurology, cardiology, ophthalmology, and exotic small animal medicine.

All states and provinces in the United States and Canada require

A veterinarian must keep good medical records, just as a doctor does who treats human patients.

that veterinarians be licensed before they can practice. The only exemptions are for veterinarians working for some federal agencies and some state governments. Licensing is controlled by the states and is not strictly uniform, although all states require successful completion of the DVM degree—or equivalent education—and passage of a national board examination. The Educational Commission for Foreign Veterinary Graduates (ECFVG) grants certification to individuals trained outside the United States who demonstrate that they meet specified requirements for the English language and clinical proficiency. ECFVG certification fulfills the educational requirement for licensure in all states except Nebraska. Applicants for licensure satisfy the examination requirement by passing the North American Veterinary Licensing Exam (NAVLE), which recently replaced the National Board Examination (NBE) and the Clinical Competency Test (CCT). The new NAVLE, administered on computer, takes one day to complete and consists of 360 multiple-choice questions, covering all aspects of veterinary medicine.

The NAVLE also includes visual materials designed to test diagnostic skills.

The majority of states also require candidates to pass a state *jurisprudence* examination covering state laws and regulations. Some states also do additional testing on clinical competency. Only a few states have *reciprocal* agreements, so it is difficult for a veterinarian to practice in a different state without first taking another state examination.

Forty-one states have continuing education requirements for licensed veterinarians. Requirements differ by state and may involve attending a class or otherwise demonstrating knowledge of recent medical and veterinary advances.

Most veterinarians begin as employees or partners in established practices. Despite the substantial financial investment in equipment, office space, and staff, many veterinarians with experience set up their own practice or purchase an established one.

Newly trained veterinarians can become U.S. government meat and poultry inspectors, disease-control workers, *epidemiologists*, or research assistants. They may also be commissioned officers in the U.S. Public Health Service, U.S. Army, or U.S. Air Force. A state license may be required.

Prospective veterinarians must have good *manual dexterity*. They should have an affinity for animals and the ability to get along with animal owners. Additionally, they should be able to quickly make decisions in emergencies. A career in veterinary medicine can be challenging and exciting.

Whatever career you are considering, remember that character counts nearly as much as education when it comes to preparing yourself for the future. According to character education expert Michael Josephson of the Josephson Institute of Ethics, good character depends on possessing certain core values, qualities like integrity and trustworthiness, respect and compassion, justice and fairness, courage, responsibility, self-discipline and diligence, and citizenship. These values affirm our dignity as human beings. Living out these values in our personal and professional lives is not only good for us as individuals; it is also good for the world around us. When we demonstrate these qualities in our lives, then we treat others the way we would each like to be treated.

As we will see in the chapters that follow, veterinarians don't only work with animals; they also work with people. As a result, these professionals have plenty of chances to put into practice the core qualities of a good character.

Compassion for animals is intimately connected with goodness of character and it may be confidently asserted that he who is cruel to animals cannot be a good man.

—Arthur Schopenhauer

Because animals play an important emotional role in their owners' lives, integrity and trustworthiness are essential characteristics for veterinarians to possess.

2

INTEGRITY AND
TRUSTWORTHINESS

*Sometimes speaking the
truth can be painful.*

Dr. Charles Miller had been working as a veterinarian in the small town of Linwood, Nebraska, for the past ten years. He had gotten to know most of the people in town who owned pets, and he had treated or vaccinated their pets at one time or another. He enjoyed his job very much.

However, sometimes Dr. Miller's job was not pleasant. Often, for instance, a veterinarian is faced with the decision of whether or not to put a pet permanently to sleep. This is never an easy decision for a vet to make, and it was especially hard for Dr. Miller when he had to consider telling his close friend Judy Johnson that her collie Lizzie might need to be euthanized.

Judy had a hard life, and Dr. Miller knew she depended on her dog's companionship. So his heart sank when she brought in Lizzie after she had noticed a lump on her dog's left thigh. Fearing the worst, Dr. Miller took an X ray, which showed that the lump was an ***intramuscular*** tumor the size of an orange. He drew a sample and sent it to the lab to determine if it was cancerous or not. If it was, Lizzie could be subjected to an extensive regimen of ***chemotherapy***. This would

An owner's relationship with a pet must be treated with respect based on integrity.

not only be very painful for the dog, but it would be expensive for her owner as well. Because Lizzie was 16 years old, her age would work against her if she required surgery.

While waiting for the lab results, Dr. Miller tried to make Lizzie as comfortable as possible. He knew Judy was hoping he would tell her that Lizzie could live for several more years in peace. Sadly, he knew the truth might not be so bright.

A few hours later, the tests showed that although the tumor was not cancerous, it was a **benign** tumor that would grow quickly. Without surgery it would cause the dog increasing pain— and yet Dr. Miller believed Lizzie was too old to survive the invasive surgery that would be required to remove it. He was convinced the best course of action would be to put Lizzie to sleep.

However, he was faced with a difficult ethical dilemma. On the one hand, he felt a sense of loyalty and responsibility to his friend Judy. She was emotionally fragile right now because of the personal circumstances in her life, and he feared one more crisis might be too much for her. On the other hand, if he didn't tell her the truth about Lizzie's condition, the dog would be forced to endure ever-increasing pain. What should he do?

People who value integrity and trustworthiness:

- tell the truth.
- don't withhold important information.
- are sincere; they don't deceive, mislead, or be devious and tricky.
- don't betray a trust.
- don't steal.
- don't cheat.
- stand up for beliefs about right and wrong.
- keep their promises.
- return what they have borrowed and pay their debts.
- stand by, support, and protect their families, friends, community, and country.
- don't talk behind people's backs or spread rumors.
- don't ask their friends to do something wrong.

Adapted from material from the Character Counts Coalition, 4640 Admiralty Way, Suite 1001, Marina del Rey, California 90292.

Student Requirements from the School of Veterinary Medicine, Louisiana State University

Veterinarians are expected to maintain a high degree of professional pride, personal dignity, and integrity. They accept and abide by an ethical code and recognize that the public image of a profession is a reflection of the general demeanor and collective attitude of its members. Admission of the qualified applicant to membership in the veterinary medical discipline is a privilege extended by the profession rather than an obligation to the individual following completion of a prescribed curriculum. Membership carries with it privileges and responsibilities to the profession and to the various publics that it serves.

Pets are particularly important to children.

Three Foundations for Ethical Decision-Making

Those who study *ethics* have determined three steps to take when we are faced with an ethical dilemma like Dr. Miller's. First, take into account the interests and well-being of everyone concerned. In this case, Dr. Miller had to weigh the animal's physical suffering against her human owner's emotional pain.

Second, when a character value like integrity and trustworthiness is at stake, always make the decision that will support that value. (For example, tell the truth even though it may cost you some pain.) If he applied this foundation of ethical decision-making, Dr. Miller might be obligated to tell Judy it was time to think about putting Lizzie to sleep.

And third, where two character values conflict (for instance, when telling the truth might hurt another person), choose the course of action

> An ethical dilemma is when we are faced with circumstances that force us to determine what is right and what is wrong.

Saying good-bye to an old friend is a hard decision to make.

Vets and Animal Killing

Deciding to kill an animal is always a difficult decision. But such killing is not always done only to save an animal from unnecessary pain and suffering. Research and educational course work also often require the death of many animals.

Concerned about this issue, Neil C. Wolff, DVM and Nedim C. Buyukmihci, V.M.D. founded the Association of Veterinarians for Animal Rights (AVAR) in 1981. These veterinarians were upset that the "nonhuman animals" they were trained to care for, treat, and heal in veterinary medical school were routinely being used and abused by society, sometimes for the most trivial of reasons. They recognized that the veterinary profession often supported practices contrary to the well-being of the animals. They formed the AVAR to educate the public and the veterinary profession to secure higher ideals of humanity and policy toward all "nonhuman animals."

The AVAR operates under the premise that all animals have value and interests independent of the values and interests of other animals, including human beings. As physicians protect the interests and needs of their patients, so should veterinarians.

that will lead to the greatest good for everyone concerned. Be sure to seek all possible alternatives, however; don't opt for dishonesty simply as the easiest and least painful way out of a difficult situation.

What would you do if you were in Dr. Miller's place? In this case, what course of action do you think will bring the greatest good for all concerned? If you were Judy, what would you want Dr. Miller to do?

Truth is meant to save you first, and the comfort comes afterward.

—Georges Bernanos

Not all vets work with pets—some work with marine animals.

3

RESPECT AND COMPASSION

*Respect and compassion are character
qualities we can extend to animals
as well as humans.*

D r. Jessica Porter thinks she was born to be a veterinarian. She knew when she was a young child that she wanted to devote her life to caring for sick and injured animals, and her lifelong dream has come true. When she was very small, she contracted polio and almost died. After a long hospital stay, she returned home and because she had to wear leg braces, she started relying on the family dog, a Great Dane, for companionship and comfort. The dog would let her hang all over him, and as a result, the two became very good friends. A special bond was formed between Jessica and her pet. The kindness shown her by the Great Dane gave her a deep respect for animals and a growing sense of compassion for their pain. She wanted to do whatever she could to help animals.

She grew up in New York City, but when she was ten years old, her family shipped her off to boarding school in England. Homesick and lonely, she thought about animals more than ever. When she read a book called *Circus Doctor,* she decided that when she graduated from school she would like to work as a zoo veterinarian. Eventually she went to Colorado State University in Fort Collins, Colorado, because it was one of two veterinary schools in the world to offer the programs she wanted. After graduating from veterinary school, she worked for a short time at the Denver Zoo and the North American Wildlife Center near Golden, Colorado.

While working at that wildlife center, she established a refuge for wolves. She felt respect and compassion for those animals, and helped retrain pet wolves to be wild. She was successful in helping hundreds of wolves learn to live in nature once again.

Another one of her dreams came true when she returned to England and became a veterinary resident at the London Zoo. She even traveled to Africa and Venezuela to participate in a few research trips.

A few years later she found herself working as the educational co-ordinator at the Whale Museum in Friday Harbor, Washington, where she began a new interest in whale and seal research. Friday Harbor is a small island town, and Dr. Porter fell in love with it. Soon the local residents were asking her to set up her own veterinarian practice, which she eventually did.

Her love, respect, and compassion for animals of all sizes contin-

Like any other animal, dolphins in captivity need compassionate medical care.

ued. She named her practice the Wolf Hollow Veterinary Clinic, and she treated any animal that needed help. It didn't take long before she also started treating injured wildlife, and at one time had several seal pups, a few fawns, raccoons, and several eagles as patients.

One of the biggest challenges she faced as a veterinarian came when she was asked to assist in the bird rescue operation following the 1989 Exxon oil tanker spill in Alaska. Being a part of the rescue operation meant leaving her home and practice; her responsibilities pulled her in two opposite directions. She had to decide whether her obligations to her practice and to herself weighed heavier than her sense of compassion for the animals injured by the oil spill.

Show respect and compassion for others by:

- being courteous and polite.
- accepting those who are different from yourself.
- assisting those who are mistreated by others.
- sharing with others.
- looking at a situation from the other's perspective.
- treating others as you want them to treat you.
- forgiving others.

Adapted from material from the Character Counts Coalition, 4640 Admiralty way, Suite 1001, Marina de Rey, California 90292.

In the end, she decided to go. "I feel absolute sympathy for these animals. These poor little guys are suffering so much, and they're victims of something that has nothing to do with them. They're not benefiting from human lifestyle," Dr. Porter told a reporter from the *Anchorage Daily News.* "One of the biggest problems with an oil spill is that you're going to lose about 50 percent of these animals and it hurts. It really hurts. A mammal is like a dog or a cat you can cuddle them and tell them it's all right. You can't do that to a bird." Dr. Porter and the other vets and volunteers knew that water alone would not get the birds clean enough to float and be released. They needed soft water, and Dawn dishwashing detergent is what every vet uses to clean a bird that has been affected by an oil spill.

When faced with an ethical decision, such as going to Alaska to help rescue and treat those oil-covered birds, Dr. Porter may have used

When an oil spill occurs, otters are just one animal that may be affected.

Oil spills are dangerous to marine birds and mammals, and also can harm fish and shellfish. Oil destroys the insulating ability of fur-bearing mammals, such as sea otters, and the water-repelling abilities of a bird's feathers, exposing these creatures to the cold and water. Many birds and animals also swallow oil when they try to clean themselves, which can poison them. Depending on just where and when a spill happens, hundreds or thousands of birds and mammals can be killed or injured.

five steps like these to help her reach a decision:

1. *Recognize that there is a moral issue at hand.* This is sometimes the hardest step for people to take. It may seem easier to ignore a problem and hope that it goes away by itself. But problems cannot be ignored; they must be dealt with. After the oil spill, Dr. Porter easily recognized that a moral issue was present.

The U.S. Environmental Protection Agency reports that almost 14,000 oil spills occur each year, mobilizing thousands of specially trained emergency response personnel. Although many spills are contained and cleaned up by the party responsible for the spill, some spills require assistance from local and state agencies, and occasionally, the federal government.

Oil spills are devastating to the natural environment.

When an oil spill occurs, the need for immediate response is essential for rescuing birds and marine mammals. You don't need to be a veterinarian to help, but training is needed before the accident ever occurs. The rehabilitation of oiled wildlife is a complex medical and technical procedure, and volunteers must be properly trained. Training workshops involve more than 200 hours of work.

2. *Evaluate the situation.* Before Dr. Porter could determine if she had an obligation and a duty to help, she needed to gather the answers to questions like these: What were conditions like at the oil spill? How extensive was the oil spill? What species were at risk because of the accident? How many animals would be affected? What practical skills were needed that Dr. Porter might be able to offer?

After an oil spill, even populations of the smallest living creatures may be devastated.

Character qualities like respect and compassion for all life can impel us to do what we can to help in the face of a disaster (like the oil spill that occurred here).

3. *Decide.* Once all of the facts were in, Dr. Porter made the decision to travel to Alaska to lend a hand with the oil-covered animals. Because she is passionate about her respect for all animals, this decision was not difficult for her to make.

4. *Implement.* Upon her arrival in Alaska, Dr. Porter immediately set out to save as many of the injured birds as possible. She worked hard and directed dozens of volunteers who were there to help.

5. *Monitor and modify.* Dr. Porter knew that if she didn't get all the soap out of a bird's feathers, she would have a very clean bird but one that won't float. A bird floats because its feathers form a basket around it, almost like a wet suit. When you get oil on the feathers, it interrupts that basket, and it lets cold water in, like getting a hole in a wet suit. Dr. Porter needed to continually assess the work she was doing to make sure that her efforts were of practical use to the animals at risk.

As Dr. Porter's life demonstrates, respect and compassion are not merely emotions we feel. Instead, they are forces that impel us to work hard for others. When we live our lives with respect and compassion, like Dr. Porter, we will bring concrete good to the world around us.

Compassion is the chief law of human existence.

—*Feodor Dostoevsky*

Zoo animals also need veterinarian care.

4

JUSTICE AND FAIRNESS

*When you seek justice, you need to be
careful you are most interested
in what is truly fair.*

As the head veterinarian at the Brandywine Zoo, Dr. Steve Chapman was responsible for the health and welfare of the 850 animals that were housed there, and he took his job seriously. He had two other veterinarians on staff that he supervised, and between the three of them, they were kept pretty busy. Every day was filled with checking on the various animals who needed shots or that looked ill. The zookeeper and animal handlers who were in charge of feeding the animals were required to fill out daily reports. On those reports, the staff indicated if an animal was not eating or seemed to be acting in an unusual way. Dr. Chapman and his staff would then scan the reports, looking for any animals that might need to be examined.

Until two months earlier, Dr. Chapman had been in private practice. He was still settling in at his new job, and he often wondered if his staff accepted him. They had all been close to his predecessor, who had been dismissed suddenly from the job, and Dr. Chapman sensed that some of them resented him as their new head veterinarian. He worked hard to get along with his staff, however, and he hoped time would make them more comfortable with each other. In the meantime, he tried not to step on anyone's toes.

People who value justice and fairness:

- treat all people the same (as much as possible).
- are open-minded; they are willing to listen to others' points of view and try to understand.
- consider carefully before making decisions that affect others.
- don't take advantage of others' mistakes.
- don't take more than their fair share.
- cooperate with others.
- recognize the uniqueness and value of each individual.

Adapted from material from the Character Counts Coalition, 4640 Admiralty Way, Suite 1001, Marina del Rey, California 90292.

On a busy Friday afternoon, Dr. Chapman took time to look over the daily reports. A few seconds later, he realized something was wrong that required his immediate attention. According to one of the animal handlers, two of the bear cubs had not eaten anything for the last four days. Dr. Chapman knew that the bear cubs would not survive much longer without food or medical attention.

He also wondered why the previous daily reports had not mentioned anything about the bear cubs' lack of appetite. As he pulled out the file that contained the last five days' worth of daily reports, he confirmed that no report had been filed indicating that the bear cubs were not eating. Dr. Chapman knew

Zoo veterinarians must be able to treat a variety of animals, big and small—including prairie dogs!

Bear cubs "teethe" just like human babies.

he had to get to the bottom of this, but that would have to wait. His first order of business was to take a look at the bear cubs.

After he examined the bear cubs, he determined that they both had dental trouble. Because they were young, some of their teeth were still coming in. Dr. Chapman prescribed a liquid diet for the bear cubs that would provide all the protein and nutrition they needed. He was confident that in a few days they would start eating solid foods once again.

Now Dr. Chapman had to get to the bottom of why it took so long for the daily reports to alert him to the problem. He knew one or more of the staff members had failed to report vital information. Should he find out what went wrong—and then take the appropriate disciplinary action? Or should he simply issue a memo, or hold a staff meeting, to remind everyone of how important those daily reports were to the health and well-being of the animals in the zoo? He

Excuses We Make for Unethical Behavior

- *If it's "necessary" then it's the right thing to do.* The ends do not justify the means.
- *If it's legal, it's okay.* The law sets only a minimal standard of behavior; being unkind, telling a lie to a friend, or taking more than your share of dessert are not crimes—but they are still unethical.
- *I was just doing it for you.* Sometimes we tell "white lies" or evade the truth to avoid hurting another's feelings—when in fact, although the truth may be uncomfortable, it will do the other person good to hear it.
- *I'm just fighting fire with fire; everybody does it.* The behavior of those around you does not excuse your lack of fairness or other unethical behaviors. There is no safety in numbers!
- *It doesn't hurt anyone.* We often underestimate the cost of failing to do the right thing.
- *It's okay so long as I don't gain personally.* Although our actions may help some individuals, however, other individuals—including ourselves—are sure to suffer as a consequence of our unethical behavior.
- *I've got it coming; I deserve to take more than my share because I worked more than anyone else.* The Golden Rule applies here: Would you want others to behave the same way?

Adapted from materials from the Josephson Institute of Ethics, 4640 Admiralty Way, Suite 1001, Marina del Rey, California 90292.

didn't want to make any enemies; he also wanted to be fair to every-one concerned.

He realized he was faced with an ethical dilemma: he needed to de-termine the course of action justice demanded. Dr. Chapman under-stood, however, that justice and punishment are two different concepts. He did not want to "get even" with whomever had failed to report the cubs' lack of appetite. But he did want to be fair and just to everyone concerned.

He asked himself these questions to help himself decide on a fair course of action:

Who is depending on me in this situation? (Dr. Chapman's staff were depending on him to provide them with fair leadership—and the zoo an-imals were also dependent on him to provide for their well-being.)

Who might be hurt by each possible course of action I might take? (The staff might be upset and angry if Dr. Chapman took disciplinary action against the person or persons who failed to report the cubs'

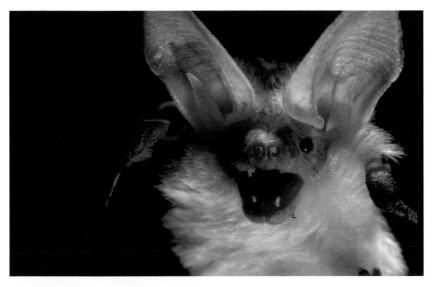

All the animals in the zoo—including bats!—depend on the veterinarian for fair, just treatment.

A Zoo Vet's Responsibilities

- Provides a preventative medicine program for all animals which includes nutrition, vaccinations, TB testing, dentistry, screenings for parasites, etc.
- Maintains medical records on all animals.
- Provides diagnostics (X rays, ultrasounds, EKGs, blood tests, etc.).
- Immobilizes animals chemically for exams, treatments, etc.
- Performs **neonatal** care, **obstetric** care, and animal autopsies.
- Participates in conservation by doing fieldwork and research on endangered species.
- Provides quarantine and preshipment exams for animals coming into or leaving the zoo.
- Maintains dialogue with other zoos and zoo vets.
- Participates in conferences and meetings for research and conservation studies.

A zoo often has its own pharmacy.

condition; if the staff is upset, Dr. Chapman may in turn find his work more difficult or uncomfortable. But if the staff fails to realize the importance of complete daily reports and a similar mistake occurs again, an animal could become sick or even die.)

What is my number one priority in this situation? (Was Dr. Chapman's job to make his staff happy? Was being happy and comfortable himself most important? Or was the zoo animals' health his first priority?)

How can I better understand this situation? (Before he took any further action, Dr. Chapman could talk with his staff to find out the circumstances behind the inadequate daily reports. By being open-minded to other perspectives on the situation, Dr. Chapman might find other fair options for handling what occurred.)

What do you think Dr. Chapman decided to do? In your opinion, what course of action is the most fair and just?

The field of zoo animal medicine has grown considerably. Today there are approximately 180 full time zoo veterinarians in the United States. As more conservation challenges lie ahead, this field of medicine will continue to grow.

Justice vs. Punishment

Justice weighs the rights of everyone concerned.
Punishment seeks to inflict suffering in return for a perceived wrong.

Justice listens to both sides.
Punishment only sees one perspective.

Justice seeks the deepest truth.
Punishment may be motivated by the desire to "get even."

Mission Statement of the American Zoo and Aquarium Association

Founded in 1924, the American Association of Zoological Parks and Aquariums, now known as the American Zoo and Aquarium Association (AZA), is a nonprofit organization dedicated to the advancement of zoos and aquariums in the areas of conservation, education, science, and recreation. AZA's vision is to work cooperatively to save and protect the wonders of the living natural world.

Over 201 zoos and aquariums throughout North America have met AZA's accreditation standards and are members of AZA. Each AZA member is unique, from the five-acre zoo to the 322,000 square-foot aquarium to the 3,000-acre wildlife center. Our members offer a rich array of animal and habitat displays for visitors to learn from and enjoy. For example, some aquariums focus strictly on freshwater aquatics, while others are renowned for their displays of saltwater habitats. AZA-accredited zoos vary widely as well, from drive-through safaris with African animals to walk-through habitats of North America species.

In addition to zoo and aquarium facilities, AZA is proud to number among its members commercial enterprises whose products and services support zoos and aquariums, nonprofit facilities that are not open to the public but are still dedicated to the health and well-being of animals and thousands of individuals. All told, there are over 6,000 caring, committed professionals, businesses and related organizations who are members of AZA.

First Female Zoo Veterinarian

In 1942 Patricia O'Connor took a position as a veterinarian at the Staten Island Zoo in New York. She received national attention, because she was the first female zoo veterinarian in the United States at the time. A graduate of the Cornell Veterinary College in Ithaca, New York, she went on to become one of the most famous and admired veterinarians in history. She kept a card file on wild animal diseases and published a book called *A Bibliography of References to Diseases in Wild Animals and Birds.* Eventually she traveled around the world and visited more than 50 countries and 100 zoos.

Justice is truth in action.

—Benjamin Disraeli

Some veterinarians treat only small animals.

5

RESPONSIBILITY

If you practice responsibility every day,
it will become a habit.

When she was only five years old, Vidya Rasheed began riding horses and collecting pets. As a youngster, she was always helping her friends care for their animals. Now, some 25 years later, she's still caring for animals. However, this time she's more than just a friend of pets; she's Dr. Vidya Rasheed, veterinarian.

Dr. Rasheed offers a mobile vet service not only for farm animals, such as horses, pigs, and goats, but she also treats domestic animals like dogs, cats, and guinea pigs. She enjoys providing a service to her community in rural Saskatchewan, Canada. Although most of the animals she treats are from the local area, when people find out she will make house calls, she also gets calls from nearby cities.

Despite having her mobile veterinarian practice for only a little over two years, Dr. Rasheed has had plenty of experience working with a wide variety of animals, in all shapes and sizes. Once she worked on a mouse in the morning, and in the afternoon found herself at a nearby zoo treating a sick elephant.

As a mobile veterinarian, Dr. Rasheed travels in her station wagon, which contains a large box holding just about everything you would find in a regular vet's office. She tries to take everything with her that she will need on a house call. In addition to a variety of drugs, vaccines,

A small-animal practice will include guinea pigs and other rodents.

and bandages, she even carries around her own portable X-ray equipment. She never knows what she will need to treat an animal.

One of the best things she likes about her job as a mobile veterinarian is that she never knows what her day will be like before she begins. She may see as many as a dozen cats and dogs on a day of routine house calls. Or she may even find herself chasing after a pig through the mud. While sometimes her work does cause her to work in conditions that are less than pleasant, like chasing pigs through the mud, she realizes that all animals deserve help when they are injured or sick.

As a veterinarian, she takes her responsibility very seriously. No matter how small the animal or how slightly they might be sick or injured, she treats each one as if they were the most important animal on the planet. Her philosophy has also led her to making preventive medicine a part of her practice as well. She believes that just like people, animals need regular checkups and vaccines. Everywhere she goes, she tells animal owners they can help keep their animals healthy through these regular checkups.

People know that Dr. Rasheed is a caring and compassionate vet, and many times they bring stray animals to her. She receives calls from people who have found animals that have been hit by cars or just abandoned; she tries to help anyone who calls her, as she feels that is her responsibility as a professional veterinarian. It is hard for her to turn away any animal, whether it is a stray or not, so she ends up treating all of them. When she takes in stray cats or dogs, she makes sure they are in good health before trying to find them good homes.

People who value responsibility:

- think before they act; they consider the possible consequences of their actions.
- accept responsibility for the consequences of their choices.
- don't blame others for their mistakes or take credit for others' achievements.
- don't make excuses.
- set a good example for others.
- pursue excellence in all they do.
- do the best with what they have.
- are dependable; others can rely on them.

Adapted from material from the Character Counts Coalition, 4640 Admiralty Way, Suite 1001, Marina del Rey, California 90292.

A small-animal practice will even treat turtles!

Veterinarians who treat people's pets may face ethical dilemmas as they try to determine their true responsibilities. For instance, pet owners may want to have their dogs' ears and tails clipped and docked—but vets may feel they have a responsibility to protect animals from unnecessary pain. According to the AVMA's position on ear cropping and tail docking, adopted on July 9, 1999: "Ear cropping and tail docking in dogs for cosmetic reasons are not medically indicated nor of benefit to the patient. These procedures cause pain and distress, and, as with all surgical procedures, are accompanied by inherent risks of anesthesia, blood loss, and infection. Therefore, veterinarians should counsel dog owners about these matters before agreeing to perform these surgeries."

Some people feel that this breed of dog looks more attractive with a docked tail and clipped ears—while others feel that these procedures are unethical.

Vets have a responsibility not only to animals but to their human owners.

Dr. Rasheed feels she has a responsibility not only to animals but to human beings as well. That's why she works with local high school students who are interested in careers in veterinary medicine. On several occasions she has allowed students to ride with her while she has made a few house calls. The students enjoy it, and it helps them with their career decision.

Sometimes Dr. Rasheed wishes she did not have quite so many responsibilities. She works hard, and like anyone, she gets tired sometimes. Once in a while, she's tempted to leave the station wagon in her driveway and sneak away in her other car where no one can find her.

But she knows people—and animals—are counting on her. That's why she takes advantage of her light days and schedules herself regular days off. She makes sure she gets eight hours of sleep a night; she eats regular, healthy meals; and she makes time for fun in her life so she won't burn out. She knows she can't be responsible to others if she doesn't take her responsibility to care for herself just as seriously.

Women in Veterinary Medicine

- Aleen Cust was the very first female graduate who completed her formal training at the Royal Veterinary college in Edinburgh, Scotland, in 1900.
- Mignon Nicholson was the very first female graduate in the United States; she attended McKillip College in 1903.
- By 1936 there were 30 women veterinarians in the United States.
- By 1963 the number of women veterinarians in the United States totaled 277.
- Today there are more than 17,000 female vets in the United States. According to a recent survey by the American Veterinarian Medical Association, in the early 1990s the number of women in veterinary medicine grew at a rate of almost six times greater than that of men.

Being responsible isn't always easy. But if you want to build a reputation as a person with good character, people must know they can count on you. You must be able to choose between what you *want* to do, and what you know you *should* do. Once you practice this choice enough times, it will become a habit that shapes your life.

Give to the world the best you have, and the best will come back to you.

—Madeline S. Bridges

Some veterinarians study wild animals like this gorilla in their natural habitats.

6

COURAGE

*Courage means you are willing to face
danger in order to achieve your life's goals.*

D r. William Karesh heads the International Field Veterinary Program for the Wildlife Conservation Society. Dr. Karesh developed
this unique program that provides veterinary services all over the world
for wildlife conservation projects. Currently a resident of New York
City, he has written a book, *Appointment at the Ends of the World:
Memoirs of a Wildlife Veterinarian*, in which he tells about his adven-
tures working and saving wild animals around the world.

Many of the animals that he has cared for in their natural habitats
had been threatened by disease and natural predators, threats which ul-
timately could lead to the extinction of a species. As a wildlife veterinarian, Dr. Karesh has worked in remote rain forests and deserts in un-
developed and politically unstable countries halfway around the world.
He has many occupational hazards, including poisonous snakes, deadly
tropical diseases, and even fire ants. He also has encountered trouble
from guerilla rebels, heavily armed soldiers, and local residents who
think he has come there to harm the animals instead of treat them. Over
the course of his career, he has worked on dangerous animals, including
buffalo and rhinos.

Dr. Karesh is not foolhardy; he takes as many safety precautions as
he possibly can. Although he enjoys his job, he knows he is putting

People who value courage:

- say what's right (even when no one agrees with them).
- do the right thing (even when it's hard).
- follow their conscience instead of the crowd.
- are willing to take risks to accomplish what needs to be done.

himself at risk, and it takes great courage to continue working with wild animals in uncertain environments. Still, his love for his job, helping wild animals when they are sick or injured, is greater than his worry about the dangers involved.

On more than one occasion, Dr. Karesh has taken part in genetic studies of a species. In one research project in which he was involved, he and a group of scientists traveled to Borneo, where they would study wild orangutans. Dr. Karesh found himself traveling through the steep hill forest and the flooded swamps in search of the orangutans. He spent many days hiking through jungles when the heat and humidity were almost unbearable.

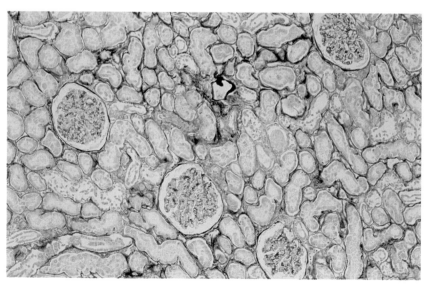

Researchers can learn much from the blood samples obtained by veterinarians like Dr. Karesh.

Orangutans are one of the largest primates.

After about a week of searching in the jungles, the team finally came across signs that orangutans were nearby. When orangutans eat fruit, nuts, or seeds, they drop bits and pieces, leaving behind a trail. At long last, one of the animals had been spotted, but that was only the beginning of another adventure: trying to figure out a way to shoot one of them with a dart gun so the researchers would get a small piece of skin to use for genetic analysis.

The orangutan would only feel a small pinch, because the researchers were using a special biopsy dart gun that had been designed and tested at the Bronx Zoo. When the dart made contact with the orangutan's body, it would cut out a small piece of skin and then fall to the ground. Dr. Karesh knew they had to be careful, since the orangutan might charge them. They could not use a tranquilizer dart, though, because if they hit an orangutan while it was high in the trees, it might fall to the ground and become injured or even die.

Finally, after days of tracking a few of the animals, Dr. Karesh's

Wild animals like this one can be dangerous—and anyone who studies them should take necessary safety precaution.

Wild animals can be unpredictable. Veterinarians—and others who are concerned about the well-being of animals—need to understand that what sometimes looks like courage may be foolishness. They need to carefully weigh what is best for everyone, including both animals and humans.

For instance, in April 2002, FedEx employees in Anchorage, Alaska were told that they should stop feeding an orphaned moose calf. The veterinarians who had become aware of the situation realized that the FedEx employees' actions could lead to a dangerous situation. According to Rick Sinnott of the Alaska Department of Fish and Game, "If it gets aggressive, the only solution we have is to destroy the moose." He continued by saying that the calf is capable of caring for itself; if it doesn't become dependent on humans, it will eventually find grass and other food to eat elsewhere. Sinnott said many people don't realize how dangerous even a young moose can be. If frightened, the animal can kick with its sharp hooves. Moose have even killed people.

group was able to safely fire the dart gun that would obtain the skin sample they needed. Then came the fun part: trying to find the darts that had fallen on the jungle floor. Sometimes the team spent a few hours searching. Finally, after a few weeks of tracking the animals and obtaining skin samples, Dr. Karesh and his party returned to civilization.

In his book, *Appointment at the Ends of the World: Memoirs of a Wildlife Veterinarian*, Dr. Karesh said of his experiences, "Out in the

When veterinarians study animal genetics, they are studying the genes that all living things possess. Genes are organized into segments along the length of a chromosome, a tightly wound spool of DNA. This spool is made up of two, complementary, single strands of DNA bound together. Every living thing has a characteristic number of chromosomes, and each chromosome carries different genes.

Genes are tightly wound spools of DNA.

Though one eats fish, has fins, and swims in the water while the other eats hamburgers, wears clothes, and walks on two feet, humans and dolphins may have more in common than people think, especially when it comes to genetics. In a Sea Grant-funded project, Texas A&M University veterinarians are comparing human chromosomes to those of dolphins and are finding that the two share many similarities.

wilds I've seen the results of dedicated people pushing to make the planet a better place for all of us, plants and animals included. I know these people, and they won't give up. Their photographs are on the huge bulletin board in my office in New York. They are ordinary human beings, like you and me, who have found their own way to contribute. They also knew a secret: Each one of us can make a difference."

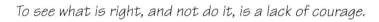

To see what is right, and not do it, is a lack of courage.

—Confucius

Becoming a vet requires self-discipline and diligence; making these character qualities a habit leads to professional success.

7

SELF-DISCIPLINE AND DILIGENCE

If you think you want to be a vet,
you need to be aware that simply
loving animals is not enough.

To be sure you know what is involved in becoming a vet, you should talk with veterinary professionals in your town. Talk to them about their careers, and ask them to tell you how much hard work and study is involved. Most vets will be more than happy to share their own experiences with you. Veterinarians have serious responsibilities, and many things in life that are worthwhile are not easy. Being a vet takes hard work, and you must have the self-discipline and diligence to go the distance. But when you do, the rewards will be great.

Linda Merry wanted those rewards. As a young person, she always thought she would become a ballerina when she grew up, but her father had encouraged her to find a profession where she could rely on her mind, and not her body, to earn a living. Her family loved animals, and when Linda graduated from high school, she decided to try veterinary medicine as a career path.

Her father supported her decision, but he reminded her that becoming a vet would take a lot of hard work. Linda knew she was up to the challenges that lay ahead. However, when they went to the advisor at the New Mexico State University, she was told she "would never make it in veterinary school." The advisor's words were all Linda needed to

Happy pet owners are one reward for a vet's diligent self-discipline.

People who value self-discipline and diligence:

- work to control their emotions, words, actions, and impulses.
- give their best in all situations.
- keep going even when the going is rough.
- are determined and patient.
- try again even when they fail the first time.
- look for ways to do their work better.

Adapted from material from the Character Education Network.

make up her mind right then and there: she would do whatever it took to become a veterinarian; she would work hard and study hard and never give up until her career goal was met.

Hard work, self-discipline, and diligence paid off for Linda, and soon she was accepted by Colorado State University College of Veterinary Medicine. She was only 19 when she started veterinary school, and by the time she graduated in 1966 there were only three women left in the program. Not everyone had been up to the challenge, and many students, both men and women, had dropped out of veterinary school after only a year or two.

Because Linda considered communication to be one of her skills, she decided to write a newspaper column called "The Merry Pet." The column was featured in several newspapers and it gave advice on many pet care questions. However, when Linda had debuted her newspaper column, the American Veterinary Medical Association (AVMA) did not allow vets to write for the public. On at least three different occasions she was brought up before the AVMA on ethics violations, but Linda was once more self-disciplined enough that she refused to give up. After further investigation, the AVMA found that the columns in question were completely ethical. Today, of course, the ban on writing for the public has been cancelled and there are hundreds, if not thousands, of articles and columns written by veterinarian professionals.

As an active member in both civic and veterinary organizations, Linda has worked hard to promote the status of veterinary medicine and

The American Veterinary Medical Association works to ensure quality performance across the field of veterinary medicine.

"The shift in gender division in our profession parallels the increasing emphasis of veterinary medicine to improve human health and well-being, as well as that of animals," says Dr. Mary Beth Leininger, president of the American Veterinarian Medical Association. "That women now have greater visibility opens a perceptual door—things are different than they used to be in veterinary medicine. No longer is it necessary to have great physical strength or come from a farm background to be an important, contributing member of our profession. Veterinary medicine requires knowledge, skill, commitment and dedication, and welcomes all who possess those characteristics."

Today, the field of veterinarian medicine is open to both men and women.

These puppies represent some of the joys of being a veterinarian.

women. Through her self-discipline and diligence, she became the first woman to lead the American Animal Hospital Association, a professional organization that has nearly 12,000 small animal practitioners and is the second largest organization in veterinary medicine.

How about you? Are you ready to work hard to become a veterinary professional? Do you think you have the necessary self-discipline and diligence? Ask yourself these questions:

Am I the type of person who can set goals and work toward completing them, no matter how many obstacles might get in my way?

Am I the type of person who is willing to forego my own pleasure and immediate gratification for the greater good?
Am I the type of person who can set limits and boundaries?

If you answered yes to those questions, then you possess one of the most important elements of good character: self-discipline and diligence.

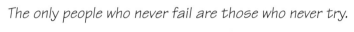

The only people who never fail are those who never try.

—Ilka Chase

Vets are in a position to be good citizens by helping to make their communities better places to live.

8

CITIZENSHIP

*Citizenship means you use your good
character to make a difference
in your community.*

Dr. Stan Coe is a veterinarian from Seattle, Washington, who recently won an award for volunteer service to the community. He received the "Weldon B. Gibson Distinguished Volunteer Award," which was established in 1981 to recognize an individual who has demonstrated sustained, exemplary service and achievement on behalf of the Washington State Foundation and the Washington State University.

In a press release to the media, a representative of Washington State University said that "Dr. Coe was being honored because he was always willing to go the extra mile in supporting leadership in volunteerism. Dr. Coe is an inspirational person, and his leadership in volunteerism is a great example for others. Although he is a very busy veterinarian, he always finds time to help others."

Veterinarians like Dr. Coe are doing their part to help make a difference in their community and town. They have embraced the spirit of volunteerism, and truly believe that the volunteer work they perform is helping not only animals but people as well.

That's what citizenship is all about. It means you are willing to get involved in service to your community and country. There are plenty of other examples of veterinarians who have been helping to make their communities a better place to live by volunteering their expertise in animal shelters and other places they are needed.

For example, Dr. Beth Logan of the Norton Road Vet Clinic near Columbus, Ohio, was selected as one of the winners of this year's National Best Vets competition held by the American Society for the Prevention of Cruelty to Animals (ASPCA). Dr. Logan was nominated for the ASPCA award by Kellie DiFrischia, Codirector of Columbus Dog Connection and is the primary vet for the rescue group. "Dr. Logan has been very supportive of our rescue efforts," says DiFrischia. "She chose Columbus Dog Connection as her philanthropic interest group. We would not be able to save as many dogs as we do without the cooperation of Dr. Logan and the entire staff at Norton Road. They are an important part of the Columbus Dog Connection team. Dr. Logan is one of a handful of vets in Columbus who practice early **spay/neuter**. That is critical for a rescue group like us because we can say with complete

Many vets volunteer their expertise in animal shelters for strays.

Spaying and neutering helps prevent kittens and puppies who are unwanted and uncared for.

confidence that no dog or puppy leaves our care able to contribute to the overpopulation problem. We would like to see all animal shelters and rescue groups practicing early spay/neuters." Dr. Logan was also recently listed as one of the top five vets in the Columbus area. This survey was taken by WBNS TV who surveyed hundreds of Central Ohio vets to see who they'd take their pets to in an emergency.

Voices for Animals is an organization in Virginia that presents awards to local veterinarians every year. The Compassionate Veterinarian Award was recently presented to two local vets, Dr. Michael Rose of Monticello Animal Hospital, and Dr. William Hay of Airport Animal Clinic, for their extensive ***pro bono*** work on behalf of local spay and neuter programs and animal shelters.

Since opening Monticello Animal Hospital in the spring of 1998, Dr. Rose and his staff have performed over 500 low-cost spay/neuter surgeries on stray cats through the Voices for Animals *feral* cat project. Dr. Rose and his staff regularly organize low-cost vaccination clinics in

According to the Character Counts Coalition, citizenship is:

- playing by the rules.
- obeying the law.
- doing your share.
- respecting authority.
- keeping informed about current events.
- voting.
- protecting your neighbors and community.
- paying your taxes.
- giving to others in your community who are in need.
- volunteering to help.
- protecting the environment.
- conserving natural resources for the future.

low-income areas; foster and adopt out homeless felines and canines at their clinic; and provide discount services for several other local animal rescue groups and shelters.

Likewise, since opening his Airport Animal Clinic in August 1998, Dr. William Hay has shown tremendous dedication to helping homeless and sick animals through his work with numerous local animal rescue groups and shelters. For the past two and a half years, Dr. Hay has worked with Voices for Animals to combat the feline overpopulation problem in his area and performed over 200 discount spay/neuter surgeries on stray and feral cats.

Kittens like these are cute—but feline overpopulation is a problem across many parts of North America.

By taking care of our pets, vets enrich the lives of us all.

Veterinarian of the Year Award

Many organizations have Veterinarian of the Year Awards to honor professionals who have volunteered their time to provide services. For example, a recipient of the Idaho Veterinarian of the Year:

- must be recognized as an outstanding veterinarian by his or her colleagues in the veterinary community.
- should also be a contributor to his or her community.

In addition, the award is given in recognition of at least one of the following criteria:

- an accumulation of accomplishments to veterinary medicine over a period of several years.
- a single outstanding identifiable contribution to veterinary medicine within the preceding five years.
- outstanding expertise within a specific branch of veterinary medicine as recognized by his or her peers.
- an outstanding contribution to society outside the field of veterinary medicine.

Veterinarians like these are good citizens who make a positive difference in their communities. What about you? You don't have to wait to be an educated professional to offer something back to your community. You don't even have to wait to be an adult. What do you have to offer right now?

In every community, there is work to be done. In every nation, there are wounds to heal. In every heart, there is the power to do it.

—Marianne Williamson

Stables require frequent visits from a veterinarian.

9

CAREER OPPORTUNITIES

*Life offers many opportunities from which
to choose. The choice is up to you.*

In the previous chapters, you have learned some interesting facts and stories about veterinary medicine and what it takes to succeed as a veterinarian in today's world. By learning as much as you can about the veterinarian profession, it will be easier for you to decide if this career is right for you . . . and if so, what type of veterinarian career would suit you best.

Employment of veterinarians is expected to grow faster than average for all occupations through the year 2010. Job openings stemming from the need to replace veterinarians who retire or otherwise leave the labor force will be almost as numerous as new jobs resulting from employment growth over the 2000–2010 period.

Most veterinarians practice in animal hospitals or clinics and care primarily for companion animals. The number of dogs as pets is expected to increase more slowly during the years ahead than in the previous decade; however, faster growth of the cat population is expected to increase the demand for feline medicine and veterinary services, offsetting any reduced demand for veterinary care for dogs. Also, as income generally increases with age, those who own pets may be more inclined to seek veterinary services. In addition, pet owners are becoming more aware of the availability of advanced care and may increas-

> ## What Are Your Values?
>
> To clarify your values, ask yourself:
>
> - What do I believe in?
> - What governs my life?
> - What do I stand for?
> - What puts meaning into my life?
> - What qualities are important for my life to be complete?
>
> Take the time to determine exactly what values are important to you. Your personal convictions, not those of others, will determine how you live.

ingly take advantage of nontraditional veterinary services, such as preventive dental care, and may more willingly pay for intensive care treatment than in the past. Finally, new technologies and medical advancements should permit veterinarians to offer better care to animals.

New graduates continue to be attracted to small animal medicine because they prefer to deal with pets and to live and work near highly populated areas. This situation will not necessarily limit the ability of veterinarians to find employment or to set up and maintain a practice in a particular area. Rather, beginning veterinarians may take positions requiring evening or weekend work to accommodate the extended hours of operation that many practices are offering. Some veterinarians take

> Median annual earnings of veterinarians were $60,910 in 2000. The middle 50 percent earned between $47,020 and $84,220. The lowest 10 percent earned less than $36,670, and the highest 10 percent earned more than $128,720.

According to a survey by the American Veterinary Medical Association, average starting salaries of 2000 veterinary medical college graduates varied by type of practice as follows:

Small animal, predominant	$42,918
Small animal, exclusive	42,640
Large animal, exclusive	41,629
Large animal, predominant	41,439
Mixed animal	40,358
Horses	28,526

Farmers depend on vets to help them keep their animals healthy.

Veterinarians held about 59,000 jobs in the United States in the year 2000. About 28 percent were self-employed in solo or group practices. Most others were employees of another veterinary practice. The federal government employed about 800 civilian veterinarians, chiefly in the U.S. Departments of Agriculture and Health and Human Services. Other employers of veterinarians are state and local governments, colleges of veterinary medicine, medical schools, research laboratories, animal food companies, and pharmaceutical companies. A few veterinarians work for zoos; but most veterinarians caring for zoo animals are private practitioners who contract with zoos to provide services, usually on a part-time basis.

Some vets may care for elephants—and some for mice!

Veterinarians can contribute to human as well as animal health. A number of veterinarians work with physicians and scientists as they research ways to prevent and treat human health problems, such as cancer, AIDS, and alcohol or drug abuse. Some determine the effects of drug therapies, antibiotics, or new surgical techniques by testing them on animals.

Some veterinarians are involved in food safety at various levels. Veterinarians who are livestock inspectors check animals for transmissible diseases, advise owners on treatment, and may quarantine animals. Veterinarians who are meat, poultry, or egg product inspectors examine slaughtering and processing plants, check live animals and carcasses for disease, and enforce government regulations regarding food purity and sanitation.

salaried positions in retail stores offering veterinary services. Self-employed veterinarians usually have to work hard and long to build a sufficient client base.

The number of jobs for large animal veterinarians is expected to grow slowly, because productivity gains in the agricultural production industry mean demand for fewer veterinarians than before to treat food animals. Nevertheless, job prospects may be better for veterinarians who specialize in farm animals than for small animal practitioners, because most veterinary medical college graduates do not have the desire to work in rural or isolated areas.

Continued support for public health and food safety, international and national disease control programs, and biomedical research on human health problems will contribute to the demand for veteri-

In Canada, most veterinarians have an income that is above the national average; a new veterinarian in private practice usually makes between $40,000 and $50,000 (Canadian).

Veterinarians help children learn more about animals.

In Canada, 40 percent of the 8,000 veterinarians practice in companion animal clinics, while one third of all Canadian veterinarians work with food-producing animals and are involved in the inspection, care, and treatment of farm livestock species. Veterinarians are an important part of the Canadian public health system, providing expertise in the area of outbreak identification and control, such as with the West Nile virus and rabies virus. Veterinarians also help to ensure food safety for humans during food production from animal sources.

narians, although such positions are few in number. However, anticipated budget cuts in the federal government may lead to low funds for some programs, limiting job growth. Veterinarians with training in public health and epidemiology should have the best opportunities for a career in the federal government.

> Love of animals is a universal impulse, a common ground on which all of us may meet. By loving and understanding animals, perhaps we humans shall come to understand each other.
> —Dr. Louis J. Camuti, first U.S. veterinarian to devote his practice to felines only.

A career in veterinary medicine can be a rewarding and exciting experience. Read as much as you can about people who have made their career as veterinarians. Talk with local vets in your hometown and see what advice they can offer you. But whatever level of veterinary medicine you choose to become involved with, don't forget that if you choose this career, you can make a positive difference in the world. Just remember: character counts!

At a 1997 symposium of the Association of Women's Veterinarians, Dr. Beth Leininger said this about vets:

Whether it is because animals present a constant manifestation of man's interconnectedness with the natural world, or because of animal's inherent acceptance of the cycle of life, people who are drawn to the veterinary profession seem to be more empathetic, more altruistic, more in touch with our "humane-ness" than most people. That seems to translate into a core understanding of the importance of the people/animal link and a recognition that regardless of the practice field we fill, we are always serving people.

How Did I Live Today?

Thomas Shanks, S.J., Ph.D., Executive Director of the Markkula Center for Applied Ethics, recommends that everyone ask themselves these five questions at the end of the day:

- Did I practice any virtues (e.g., integrity, honesty, compassion)?
- Did I do more good than harm?
- Did I treat others with dignity and respect?
- Was I fair and just?
- Was my community better because I was in it? Was I better because I was in my community?

There is only one of you in the world, just one, and if that is not fulfilled then something has been lost.

—Martha Graham

FURTHER READING

Josephson, Michael S. and Wes Hanson, editors. *The Power of Character.* San Francisco: Jossey-Bass, 1998.

Karesh, William. *Appointment at the Ends of the World: Memoirs of a Wildlife Veterinarian.* New York: Warner, 1999.

Kidder, Rushworth M. *How Good People Make Tough Choices.* New York: Simon & Schuster, 1995.

Lee, Mary Price. *Opportunities in Animal and Pet Care Careers.* Lincolnwood, Ill.: VGM Career Horizons: 1994.

Swope, Robert. *Opportunities in Veterinary Medicine Careers.* Lincolnwood, Ill.: VGM Career Horizons, 1993.

FOR MORE INFORMATION

American Veterinary Medical Association
1931 N. Meacham Rd.
Suite 100
Schaumburg, IL 60173-4360
www.avma.org

Animal Concerns
5801 Beacon Street, Suite 2
Pittsburgh, PA 15217
envirolink.org

Association of American Veterinary Medical Colleges
1101 Vermont Ave., NW
Suite 710
Washington, DC 20005
www.aavmc.org

Association of Veterinarians for Animal Rights
P.O. Box 208
Davis, CA 95612
avar.org

Canadian Veterinarian Medical Association
339 Booth Street
Ottawa, ON
K1R 7K1 Canada
cvma-acmv.org

Character Education Network
www.charactered.net

Josephson Institute of Ethics
www.josephsoninstitute.org

GLOSSARY

Agribusiness The business of farming and agriculture.

Benign Not cancerous.

Cesarean section A surgery that removes a baby from its mother through the abdominal wall.

Chemotherapy The use of chemicals for treating disease (particularly cancer).

Epidemiologists A branch of medical science that deals with the incidence, distribution, and prevention of a disease in an entire population (rather than in individuals).

Ethics The study of right and wrong.

Euthanize To kill a hopelessly sick animal or individual for reasons of mercy.

Feral Wild.

Intramuscular Within the muscle.

Jurisprudence A system of law.

Manual dexterity The ability to use one's hands well.

Neonatal Having to do with conditions occurring immediately after birth.

Neuter To remove the reproductive ability from a male animal.

Obstetric Having to do with birth and pregnancy.

Pro bono Work that is done for free as a donation to the community.

Reciprocal Having to do with a mutual agreement by two parties to honor each other's licensing or regulations.

Spay To remove the ovaries from a female animal so that she cannot have babies.

INDEX

BIOGRAPHIES

Rae Simons has ghostwritten hundreds of books, helping authors write more clearly. She is also the author of three novels.

John Riddle is the author of 15 books and a speaker and presenter at many writers' conferences around the country.

Cheryl Gholar is a Community and Economic Development Educator with the University of Illinois Extension. She has a Ph.D. in Educational Leadership and Policy Studies from Loyola University, and she has more than 20 years of experience with the Chicago Public Schools as a teacher, counselor, guidance coordinator, and administrator. Recognized for her expertise in the field of character education, Dr. Gholar assisted in developing the K–12 Character Education Curriculum for the Chicago Public Schools, and she is a five-year participant in the White House Conference on Character Building for a Democratic and Civil Society. The recipient of numerous awards, she is also the author of *Beyond Rhetoric and Rainbows: A Journey to the Place Where Learning Lives.*

Ernestine G. Riggs is an Assistant Professor at Loyola University Chicago and a Senior Program Consultant for the North Central Regional Educational Laboratory. She has a Ph.D. in Educational Leadership and Policy Studies from Loyola University, and she has been involved in the field of education for more than 35 years. An advocate of teaching the whole child, she is a frequent presenter at district and national conferences; she also serves as a consultant for several state boards of education. Dr. Riggs has received many citations, including an award from the United States Department of Defense Overseas Schools for Outstanding Elementary Teacher of America.